Major European Union Nations

Major
European Union
Nations

Austria
Belgium
Czech Republic
Denmark
France
Germany
Greece
Ireland

Italy
The Netherlands
Poland
Portugal
Spain
Sweden
United Kingdom

AUSTRIA

Jeanine Sanna and Shaina C. Indovino

Mason Crest

Mason Crest
370 Reed Road, Broomall,
Pennsylvania 19008
www.masoncrest.com

Printed in the Hashemite Kingdom of Jordan.

First printing
9 8 7 6 5 4 3 2 1

Library of Congress Cataloging-in-Publication Data

Sanna, Jeanine.
  Austria / by Jeanine Sanna and Shaina C. Indovino.
    p. cm. — (The European Union : political, social, and economic cooperation)
  Includes bibliographical references and index.
  ISBN 978-1-4222-2232-4 (hardcover) — ISBN 978-1-4222-2231-7 (series hardcover) — ISBN 978-1-4222-9262-4 (ebook)
  1. Austria—Juvenile literature. 2. European Union—Austria—Juvenile literature. I. Indovino, Shaina Carmel. II. Title.
  DB17.S26 2012
  943.6—dc22
                                    2010051075

Produced by Harding House Publishing Services, Inc.
www.hardinghousepages.com
Interior layout by Micaela Sanna.
Cover design by Torque Advertising + Design.

CONTENTS

AUSTRIA
European Union Member since 1995

Grnünd

Krems

Linz

Wels

St. Pölten

Steyr

Baden

★ **Vienna**

Eisenstadt

Wiener
Neustadt

Salzburg

Bregenz

Kufstein

Bischofshofen

Bruck

Leoben

Innsbruck

Feldkirch

Landeck

Badgastein

Graz

Lienz

Klagenfurt

Villach

INTRODUCTION

Sixty years ago, Europe lay scarred from the battles of the Second World War. During the next several years, a plan began to take shape that would unite the countries of the European continent so that future wars would be inconceivable. On May 9, 1950, French Foreign Minister Robert Schuman issued a declaration calling on France, Germany, and other European countries to pool together their coal and steel production as "the first concrete foundation of a European federation." "Europe Day" is celebrated each year on May 9 to commemorate the beginning of the European Union (EU).

The EU consists of twenty-seven countries, spanning the continent from Ireland in the west to the border of Russia in the east. Eight of the ten most recently admitted EU member states are former communist regimes that were behind the Iron Curtain for most of the latter half of the twentieth century.

Any European country with a democratic government, a functioning market economy, respect for fundamental rights, and a government capable of implementing EU laws and policies may apply for membership. Bulgaria and Romania joined the EU in 2007. Croatia, Serbia, Turkey, Iceland, Montenegro, and Macedonia have also embarked on the road to EU membership.

While the EU began as an idea to ensure peace in Europe through interconnected economies, it has evolved into so much more today:

- Citizens can travel freely throughout most of the EU without carrying a passport and without stopping for border checks.

- EU citizens can live, work, study, and retire in another EU country if they wish.

- The euro, the single currency accepted throughout seventeen of the EU countries (with more to come), is one of the EU's most tangible achievements, facilitating commerce and making possible a single financial market that benefits both individuals and businesses.

- The EU ensures cooperation in the fight against cross-border crime and terrorism.

- The EU is spearheading world efforts to preserve the environment.

- As the world's largest trading bloc, the EU uses its influence to promote fair rules for world trade, ensuring that globalization also benefits the poorest countries.

- The EU is already the world's largest donor of humanitarian aid and development assistance, providing around 60 percent of global official development assistance to developing countries in 2011.

The EU is not a nation intended to replace existing nations. The EU is unique—its member countries have established common institutions to which they delegate some of their sovereignty so that decisions on matters of joint interest can be made democratically at the European level.

Europe is a continent with many different traditions and languages, but with shared values such as democracy, freedom, and social justice, cherished values well known to North Americans. Indeed, the EU motto is "United in Diversity."

Enjoy your reading. Take advantage of this chance to learn more about Europe and the EU!

Ambassador John Bruton,
Former EU President and Prime Minister of Ireland

Salzburg, Austria.

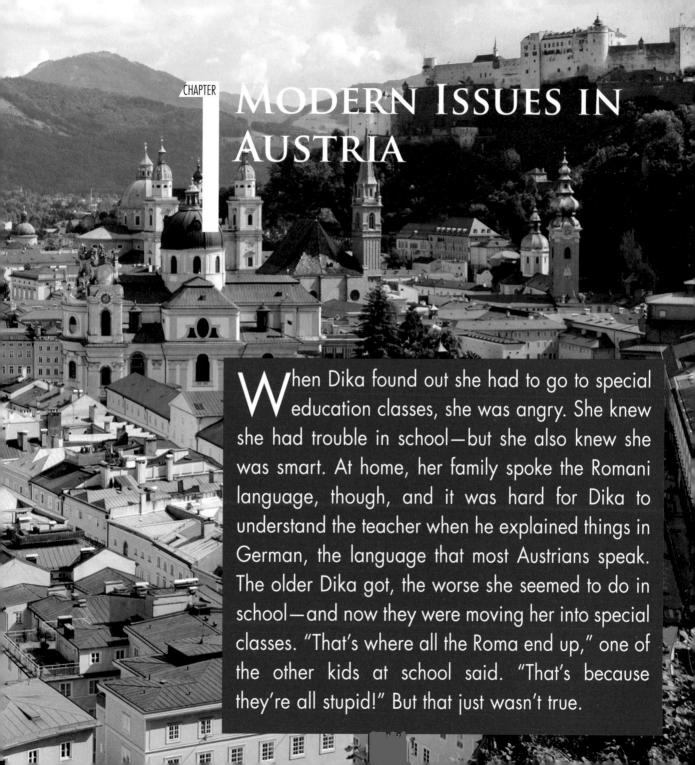

CHAPTER 1

MODERN ISSUES IN AUSTRIA

When Dika found out she had to go to special education classes, she was angry. She knew she had trouble in school—but she also knew she was smart. At home, her family spoke the Romani language, though, and it was hard for Dika to understand the teacher when he explained things in German, the language that most Austrians speak. The older Dika got, the worse she seemed to do in school—and now they were moving her into special classes. "That's where all the Roma end up," one of the other kids at school said. "That's because they're all stupid!" But that just wasn't true.

The Formation of the European Union (EU)

The EU is a confederation of European nations that continues to grow. As of 2012, there are twenty-seven official members. Several other candidates are also waiting for approval. All countries that enter the EU agree to follow common laws about foreign security policies. They also agree to cooperate on legal matters that go on within the EU. The European Council meets to discuss all international matters and make decisions about them. Each country's own concerns and interests are important, though. And apart from legal and financial issues, the EU tries to uphold values such as peace, human dignity, freedom, and equality.

All member countries remain autonomous. This means that they generally keep their own laws and regulations. The EU becomes involved only if there is an international issue or if a member country has violated the principles of the union.

The idea for a union among European nations was first mentioned after World War II. The war had devastated much of Europe, both physically and financially. In 1950, the French foreign minister suggested that France and West Germany combine their coal and steel industries under one authority. Both countries would have control over the industries. This would help them become more financially stable. It would also make war between the countries much more difficult. The idea was interesting to other European countries as well. In 1951, France, West Germany, Belgium, Luxembourg, the Netherlands, and Italy signed the Treaty of Paris, creating the European Coal and Steel Community. These six countries would become the core of the EU.

In 1957, these same countries signed the Treaties of Rome, creating the European Economic Community. In 1965, the Merger Treaty formed the European Community. Finally, in 1992, the Maastricht Treaty was signed. This treaty defined the European Union. It gave a framework for expanding the EU's political role, particularly in the area of foreign and security policy. It would also replace national currencies with the euro. The next year, the treaty went into effect. At that time, the member countries included the original six plus another six who had joined during the 1970s and '80s.

In the following years, the EU would take more steps to form a single market for its members. This would make joining the union even more of an advantage. Three more countries joined during the 1990s. Another twelve joined in the first decade of the twenty-first century. As of 2012, six countries were waiting to join the EU.

Flags outside of the European Union headquarters.

Dika knows her country has lots of problems. **Discrimination** against Dika's people is just one of the those problems. But she also knows Austria has many strengths. She's made up her mind that when she grows up she will help Austria be an even better country, a strong member of the European Union where kids like her will have the same chances to learn that everyone else does.

THE ROMA IN AUSTRIA

Dika and her family are Roma, an ancient group of people that are sometimes called Gypsies. Somewhere between 10,000 and 25,000 Romani-speaking people live in Austria. They are the only ethnic group that is officially recognized throughout Austria.

Most of the Roma in Austria live in the cities. Many are self-employed in secondhand trading and other businesses. And like Dika, many of them face big challenges when they go to school. Only a few of them stay in school long enough to graduate, and even fewer go on to higher education.

But people in Austria are working to make things better for children like Dika. Special teaching materials are being developed, and Roma teaching assistants have been assigned to some schools. Language classes are being held to teach both children and adults German.

Roma leaders are speaking out for their people. They insist that the Roma need to be represented in the government, both in Austria and in the EU as a whole. That is the only way they can help shape political, social, and educational systems that will be fair to them.

THE HISTORY OF THE ROMA IN AUSTRIA

The Roma have lived in the land we now know as Austria since the end of the fourteenth century. They made their living as blacksmiths, knife-grinders, broom makers, seasonal farm workers, and musicians. People liked the Roma's skills—but they also distrusted the Roma. During the eighteenth century, they were persecuted and their children were taken away from them and sent to live with non-Roma families. They were forced to live on the edge of villages in "gypsy houses," which still exist.

In the twentieth century, things got even worse for the Roma. When Hitler came into control, he deported them to concentration camps. Many of them died there. After the war, those who survived or managed to escape faced better conditions. Some of them worked in the construction and metal industries, while others were carpenters, electricians, and mechanics.

ROMA, AUSTRIA, AND THE EU

While the Roma in Austria are still struggling for equality, conditions are even worse for

A Roma demonstration to gain equality.

Roma in other EU nations. The Roma are a big issue throughout the European Union. Does the EU have the right to decide how they should be treated? Or should each member nation have the right to make their own policies regarding the Roma? These are not easy questions for the EU to answer.

In 2010, France deported many Roma, forcing them to leave the country. When the EU condemned France for its actions, the French European Affairs minister responded by saying, "That's not the way to speak to a great state." Austrian Chancellor Werner Faymann was quick to hit back at France, insisting that all EU member nations be treated equally, regardless of their size. Individual nations cannot decide to make their own laws that go against EU treaties that protect the rights of Roma and other groups. "This applies to France as much as to smaller or medium-sized countries: there can't be two different standards here," said Faymann. Other Austrians joined in, condemning France's stance.

Most Austrians believe the countries that are members of the EU need to abide by the EU's laws regarding the Roma. No matter how big or small the nation, it should follow the EU's policies, rather than making its own.

WHO HAS THE POWER?

One of the big issues in the EU is similar to one that the United States faces as well: who should have more power, the central government (the EU in Europe, or Washington, D.C., in the United States) or the individual members (the nations of Europe or the states of the United States)? This issue becomes obvious when smaller issues arise. In the United States, it came to a head in the 1800s over the issue of slavery, causing the Civil War, but it continues to be an important question whenever states don't agree on a particular issue, such as same-sex marriage or abortion rights. The smaller issues in Europe are different (they have to do with the Roma, with immigration, and with money), but the big issue is very much the same. Will the EU be able to unite its power the way the United States did—or will it continue to act as separate nations?

MUSLIMS IN AUSTRIA

Muslims are another group of people in the EU who, like the Roma, often face discrimination. Their situation in Austria, however, is better than it is in many other EU nations.

In 2010, between 400,000 and 500,000 Muslims lived in Austria, about 6 percent of the entire population. Most Muslims came to Austria during the 1960s as migrant workers from Turkey, Bosnia, and Serbia. Some communities came from Arab nations and Pakistan.

MUSLIMS IN THE EUROPEAN UNION

Muslims are people who follow Islam, a religion that grew from some of the same roots as Judaism and Christianity. "Islam" means "submission to God," and Muslims try to let God shape all aspects of their lives. They refer to God as Allah; their holy scriptures are called the Qur'an, and they consider the Prophet Muhammad to be their greatest teacher.

About 16 million Muslims live in the European Union—but their stories vary from country to country. Some Muslim populations have been living in Europe for hundreds of years. Others came in the middle of the twentieth century. Still others are recent refugees from the troubled Middle East. By 2020, the Muslim population in Europe is predicted to double. By 2050, one in five Europeans are likely to be Muslim, and by 2100, Muslims may make up one-quarter of Europe's people.

Not all Europeans are happy about these predictions. Negative stereotypes about Muslims are common in many EU countries. Some Europeans think all Muslims are terrorists. But stereotypes are dangerous!

When you believe a stereotype, you think that people in a certain group all act a certain way. "All jocks are dumb" is a stereotype. "All women are emotional" is another stereotype, and another is, "All little boys are rough and noisy." Stereotypes aren't true! And when we use stereotypes to think about others, we often fall into prejudice—thinking that some groups of people aren't as good as others.

Fundamentalist Muslims want to get back to the fundamentals—the basics—of Islam. However, their definition of what's "fundamental" is not always the same as other Muslims'. Generally speaking, they are afraid that the influence of Western morals and values will be bad for Muslims. They believe that the laws of Islam's holy books should be followed literally. Many times, they are willing to kill for their beliefs—and they are often willing to die for them as well. Men and women who are passionate about these beliefs have taken part in violent attacks against Europe and the United States. They believe that terrorism will make the world take notice of them, that it will help them fight back against the West's power.

But most Muslims are not terrorists. In fact, most Muslims are law-abiding and hardworking citizens of the countries where they live. Some Muslims, however, believe that women should have few of the rights that women expect in most countries of the EU. This difference creates tension, since the EU guarantees women the same rights as men.

But not all Muslims are so conservative and strict. Many of them believe in the same "golden rule" preached by all major religions: "Treat everyone the way you want to be treated."

But despite this, hate crimes against Muslims are increasing across the EU. These crimes range from death threats and murder to more minor assaults, such as spitting and name-calling. Racism against Muslims is a major problem in many parts of the EU. The people of the European Union must come to terms with the fact that Muslims are a part of them now. Terrorism is the enemy to be fought—not Muslims.

Muslim women in Austria are allowed to wear the traditional veils at work and public school.

Ever since 1867, however, Muslims in Austria have had the right to build mosques and practice their religion. Muslims occupy good positions within the Austrian civil service, and Austrian law gives them various rights and privileges, including the right to organize and manage their community affairs independently through municipal councils. The Austrian government acknowledges the Islamic Religious Body as a corporation under public law. About two hundred teachers give Islamic religious education at public schools according to the nationally approved curricula. Muslim girls and women can wear the veil at work, in public ceremonies, and in public schools. (This is not the case in other EU nations, such as France, where Muslim women are not allowed to wear their traditional head coverings in public places.)

AUSTRIA AND IMMIGRATION

Because Austria is a member of the European Union, people from other countries in the EU can move freely across its borders. As a country bordered by eight others, immigration issues are important to Austria.

Until recently, Austria's border with Hungary was closed. If people from Hungary tried to immigrate to Austria, the military would deport them. Now, however, Hungary is a member of the EU, and so Austria must allow people to enter freely across the border it shares with Hungary. This is a concern for Austria, because Hungary is a transit country for illegal immigrants who pass through from non-EU countries in Eastern Europe. The Austrian government worries that Hungary does not have laws in place, nor the power to enforce the laws it does have, to control the movement of illegal immigrants and criminal **trafficking** into Austria.

Austria is also concerned about the 200,000 to 300,000 Turkish immigrants who live in Austria. Most of the Turks were hired as "guest workers" back in 1964 for the construction and export industries. More later came to Austria as refugees during the 1970s. In 1973, however, the Austrian government began to pass laws to restrict Turkish immigrants. More restrictions were put into place in 1997, and the most recent restrictions were made in 2006. Although Islam is accepted in Austria, many Austrians fear that the Muslims from Turkey will be Islamic **radicals** who are involved with terrorism. Austrians are increasingly prejudiced against Turkish people and culture, and Austria has tried to block Turkey from becoming a member of the EU. Despite this, the Austrian government has made efforts since 2005 to help Turkish immigrants and their descendants gain rights equal to those of naturally born, ethnic Austrians.

FINANCES, AUSTRIA, AND THE EU

Money is another big issue that sometimes divides the nations of the EU. In 2008, a financial **recession** hit most of the entire world, including the EU. Some European countries

Austrian children learning how to ski—a common sport in Austria.

were affected worse than others, though. This meant that the richer nations were expected to help the ones that were in financial trouble. In 2010, they bailed out Greece, one of the nations that was in the biggest trouble. In return, Greece was expected to cut spending and raise taxes.

But later in the year, Greece had still not met the commitments it had made to the European Union in return for the massive bailout package it had received. As a result, Austria refused to give its aid installment of some 190 million euros ($258 million) to Greece. "Very clear conditions were laid down in return for the EU aid to Greece. But

as things currently stand, Greece has not kept to the plan," the Austrian finance minister told reporters.

Once again, Austria was firmly in favor of giving power to EU's centralized government—and using money as a way to enforce that power.

INTERNATIONAL AFFAIRS

Because eight different countries surround Austria, there is bound to be international tension once in a while. During the past few years, this tension has involved the Czech Republic, another member of the European Union. Austrians became outspoken about a nuclear power plant in Temelín, a small village in the Czech Republic which is close to the Austrian border.

Many Austrians signed a petition in 2008, suggesting that the Czech Republic should be removed from the EU unless the nuclear power plant was shut down. A significant percentage of Czech citizens were against the development of the power plant as well, but despite national and international opposition, the nuclear power plant remained open. The Czech Republic is still a member of the European Union.

Like all nations, Austria struggles with a host of issues like these. As children like Dika know, Austria faces many problems, including discrimination and prejudice—but Austria also believes in the principles of the European Union. It is working hard to support the EU and make it a stronger force in the world.

One of Austria's many historical buildings

2 AUSTRIA'S HISTORY AND GOVERNMENT

Austria has been populated for thousands of years; evidence has been found that shows humans have lived in that area since the Paleolithic Age (about 80,000 to 10,000 BCE). In 1991, the mummy of a man dating back to the Stone Age was found in the ice of the Alps, almost perfectly preserved.

Seventeenth-century map of Austria

Later on, from about 800 to 400 BCE, many **Celtic** tribes inhabited Austria, trading with others from all over Europe. This was a period when many groups invaded the land, partly because of the availability and convenience of the Danube River. These tribes included the Celts, as well as the Romans and others.

The Roman Empire

The Romans founded Vienna, now the capital of Austria. They settled many other towns as well and in the second century CE brought about the spread of Christianity to the region.

When the Roman Empire lost power around 470 CE, the Roman culture that had **permeated** the area disappeared. From this point on, Austria was prey to many wandering tribes and armies. Then, in the eighth century, Charlemagne established the territory as part of his Holy Roman Empire. This lasted until his death in 907, after which **anarchy** reigned until Otto the Great conquered the area in 955.

The Babenberg Dynasty

After this era, which lasted for around twenty years, a new family took control. These were the Babenbergs, whose rule lasted for more than three centuries. They were the ones who gave the region its name: Österreich or Austria.

In the thirteenth century, however, the emperor of the Holy Roman Empire invaded Austria. He refused to recognize the rule of the Babenberg king, and both sides fought. King Ottokar was killed on the battlefield, and Emperor Rudolf von Hapsburg took control, starting a dynasty that would last more than six hundred years.

Hapsburg Rule

The Hapsburgs expanded their territory; over time, the family controlled the land in Bohemia, Spain, and Hungary, as well as Austria. The empire was forced to divide because of its great size—eventually, there were two branches, one controlling the

Dating Systems and Their Meaning

You might be accustomed to seeing dates expressed with the abbreviations BC or AD, as in the year 1000 BC or the year AD 1900. For centuries, this dating system has been the most common in the Western world. However, since BC and AD are based on Christianity (BC stands for Before Christ and AD stands for *anno Domini*, Latin for "in the year of our Lord"), many people now prefer to use abbreviations that people from all religions can be comfortable using. The abbreviations BCE (meaning Before Common Era) and CE (meaning Common Era) mark time in the same way (for example, 1000 BC is the same year as 1000 BCE, and AD 1900 is the same year as 1900 CE), but BCE and CE do not have the same religious overtones as BC and AD.

area around Austria and Germany, the other in charge of Spain and Holland. However, this power would not last forever.

While the Hapsburg rulers were busy expanding their territory, they were ignoring the potential threat of the Ottomans. This group gained in power, until in 1453, they took control of Constantinople, the capital of the Holy Roman Empire. Twice they were able to invade as far as Vienna, but both times they met fierce resistance at the city limits. Finally, under Prince Eugene of Savoy, the army was able to rid the country of the Turks and take back their territory.

PROTESTANTISM

Although seemingly peaceful now, the empire still had problems to face. As **economies** based on **currency** spread, the importance of Austrian trade routes decreased. Because of economic and political instability, the **Protestant Revolution** spread rapidly in Austria. The Hapsburgs tried to undo the results of this spread of Protestantism through the Counter Revolution. This alliance between the Austrian government and the Catholic Church continued throughout the rule of the Hapsburg dynasty.

At first, it was impossible to keep the Protestants from practicing their religion, and so the rulers of Austria opted for a practice of **toleration**. However, under Ferdinand II, the strong feelings against Protestants led to the Thirty Years' War (1618–1648). After the war ended with the Peace of Westphalia, the Hapsburg

lands became their own empire, separate from the Holy Roman Empire, which gradually lost power and faded into the background.

In 1700, the last Spanish Hapsburg died. This caused many clashes between governments as many countries tried to win control of Spain. Austria lost this War of Spanish **Succession**, but it was able to keep control of its territories in Italy and the Netherlands.

At this time, the monarchy was not absolute. In other words, it left many rights to the provinces, such as taxation. However, other powers still rested in the hands of the emperor, including the **repression** of free speech and worship.

MARIA THERESA— THE FIRST QUEEN OF AUSTRIA

In 1740, Emperor Karl VI died without any male heirs. Thus, out of necessity, the crown passed to his daughter, Maria Theresa. The new empress was forced to prove herself in more than one war as she fought off those like the Prussian king Fredrich II who yearned after her lands. Throughout both the Silesian War (1740–1748) and the Seven Years' War (1756–1763), she managed to keep her territory together. The only province she lost was Silesia, which she gave up to Prussia.

Maria Theresa's husband was later elected emperor of the Holy Roman Empire. However, he was never as successful as the strong woman he married. She and her son Joseph II put into place many reforms that are still important today, includ-

Maria Theresa

ing the abolishment of **serfdom** and the **secularization** of monasteries and other church lands.

THE FRENCH REVOLUTION BRINGS NEW IDEAS

This peaceful age of monarchs lasted until the 1790s when the French Revolution brought ideas of equality and democracy to Austria. Threatened by these new ideals, Emperor Franz II, the grandson of Maria Theresa and the nephew of the French queen Marie Antoinette (who was beheaded during the revolution), took action. He joined a **coalition** against France. This might have seemed like a good idea at the time, but Austria later suffered great losses under the invasion of Napoleon Bonaparte.

The two countries became involved in a power struggle. Napoleon crowned himself emperor of France in 1804, and Franz followed his example by creating the Empire of Austria. In 1806, the Holy Roman Empire dissolved because of the Confederation of the Rhine—a group of fifteen German states who joined with France. Therefore, Franz was forced to give up his crown. From then on Napoleon was able to inflict heavy losses on Austria. He even went so far as to conquer Vienna twice. However, he, like all other men, was not indestructible. He was finally defeated at Waterloo and was exiled to the Island of Saint Helen's, where he died in 1821. The old order of monarchies was restored in Europe.

THE MONARCHY WEAKENS

Early in 1848, the idea of freedom for the middle classes again reached Austria from France. This time the people asked for **freedom of the press** as well as a **constitution**. The hated **police system** of the time was swept away, but the remainder of the revolution was stopped. Emperor Franz Joseph I put into place a system that left no room for anything except the absolute right of a monarch to rule.

Because of his rule and policy of neutrality, especially in the Crimean War (1854–1856), Austria found itself without friends or allies when it was attacked by Sardinia. Three years later, Austria was forced to give up its territory of Lombardy. With the October Diploma and the February Edict, the country also put in place a **parliament**.

The government was weakening, and reorganization was needed. In 1867, a compromise was reached that put in place a dual state: the Austro-Hungarian Empire. A cultural minority ruled the people, making other groups, especially the Slavs, unhappy.

Around this time, two political parties—the Social Democratic Party and the Christian Social Party—emerged. Both demanded civil rights for the people and were able to let their voices be heard in Austria's first general election in 1907. **Anti-Semitism** also spread at this time as many poor Jews moved to Austria from the eastern provinces of the empire. Despite these setbacks, some aspects of the culture flourished, and Vienna became a major center of the arts.

Napoleon

Modern Austria echoes the long-ago land.

Austria was relatively peaceful from this time until the beginning of World War I. It had learned from its previous mistakes and formed alliances with other countries, including the German Empire and Italy, in the Triple Alliance. However, feelings of **nationalism** were growing, causing tensions to rise. People also demanded better pay and working conditions, setting the stage for World War I to begin.

WORLD WAR

On June 28, 1914, Archduke Franz Ferdinand was assassinated. He was the heir to the Austrian throne, and his murder by a member of a nationalist group caused the tensions that had been building for years to flare into a full-fledged war.

The first three years of fighting were futile; none of the European nations emerged with a clear lead. The entrance of the United States into World War I in 1917 helped tip the scales against the Central Powers (Austria-Hungary, the German Empire, and Turkey). After the war ended, the Austro-Hungarian Empire dissolved into small nation states, which later formed the Republic of Austria.

In 1919, at the end of the war, the Treaty of Saint-Germain established fixed borders for Austria. It also made sure that the new country was forbidden to form any alliances with Germany. In the end, Austria was a small country of about 7 million people, more than a third of who lived in Vienna. While the empire had been self-sufficient, Austria now was forced to look elsewhere for raw materials, food, and markets for its goods. Because of this, the economy crashed and a period of starvation ensued. Inflation set in, which was only stopped when the League of Nations (a **precursor** to the United Nations) stepped in and helped.

SOCIALISM IN AUSTRIA

The postwar country's political views swerved as far from monarchy as is possible. Two **socialist** factions, the "Red," who were more moderate, and the "Black," who believed that the clergy should have more power, headed the new socialist views. Conflict escalated between the two groups when the Black won the 1921 election, and riots raged in the streets of Vienna. In the end, two private **militias** both posed a threat to the government. Eventually, the National Socialist Party (the Black) gained popularity, partly because of the increase in anti-Semitism.

A new chancellor, Engelbert Dollfus, came into power in 1932. He was against National Socialism; however, he believed in **fascism**. Because of this, he quickly became involved with Mussolini, the Italian fascist leader of the time. Because he was so suppressive of the socialists, a revolt occurred in 1934, but the army soon put it down. After this demonstration, all political parties were banned, and a **totalitarian** state was put into place. Dollfus was assassinated in 1934.

At this time, German influence, led by Adolph Hitler, increased in Austria. The new chancellor, Kurt von Schuschnigg, appointed the National Socialists to government posts. Finally, Hitler forced Schuschnigg to resign, and Austria was occupied by German troops in 1938.

After World War II, when Germany was **vanquished**, Austria regained its freedom when the Allies decided to reestablish Austria as an independent nation in 1943. In 1945, it was taken over by Soviet and American troops and a **provisional government** was set in place. The original constitution was restored with one major revision: the country was now divided into separate occupation zones, each controlled by a different Allied power.

RECONSTRUCTION

Now began the job of reconstructing the economy and the government. However, recovery didn't go as fast as was expected because of the decline of trade between the two halves of Europe. Eastern Europe remained communist with tension between it and the democratic Western Europe. Finally, in 1955, a formal treaty between France, Great Britain, the United States, the USSR (the Soviets), and Austria put the Austrian government back in the hands of its native citizens. There was a heavy price, though: Austria had to pay **reparations** to the USSR, as well as promise to remain neutral in all future conflicts and to never purchase or develop weapons of mass destruction. After this treaty was passed, Austria was allowed into the United Nations.

By the 1960s, Austria was back on its feet. The country had joined the European Free Trade Association in 1959, allowing it to trade without having to pay **tariffs** to the other European nations. The balance of power between the liber-

Modern Austria

Downtown modern Salzburg

als and the conservatives was about equal, with both the People's Party and the Socialists maintaining control at various times.

MODERN GOVERNMENT

In 1983, the Socialist government fell, and it joined forces with the **radical** Freedom Party. Three years later, Kurt Waldheim was elected president, despite rumors he had been involved in **atrocities** as a German officer during World War II. His election caused controversy throughout the world.

By the late 1980s, Austria had become more **capitalist** as it started to **privatize** some state-owned industries. In 1995, it entered the European Union (EU).

Today, Austria's government has three main parties: the People's Party, the Social Democrats, and the Freedom Party, which is far **right** and radical. In 2000, the People's Party and Freedom Party joined together so that a stable government could be formed, but this led to Austria being criticized by the rest of the EU because of the radical Freedom Party's involvement in the government. The Freedom Party members argued among themselves, leading to a collapse of the government. Recent elections have shown that more parties are now edging into Austria's politics, including the Green Party, which is very concerned with ecological and socioeconomic issues. Despite this, in the 2010 election, Heinz Fischer of the Social Democratic Party was reelected as the country's president. He won with an overwhelming majority of nearly 80 percent of the votes.

THE POWER OF YOUNG VOTERS

Austria's politics are increasingly influenced by Austrian youth. In 2007, all Austrians sixteen or older gained the right to vote.

Innsbruck at night

3 THE ECONOMY

After World War II, the government took control of many of Austria's industries to prevent them from coming under the control of the USSR for the payment of war reparations. Because of this, for a long time the government had a large role in the economy. In the past twenty years, however, the country has started to privatize businesses. This process has been mainly successful, although the government still owns some industries and services.

Despite being in the middle of changing hands, Austria's economy is very strong for various reasons. One of these is that now, as throughout history, Austria serves as a hub between many countries. Goods flow through the country, especially those used in fuels like oil and natural gas.

Not only goods but people as well gather in Austria. The country has been the site of countless treaty meetings and international conferences. Each time this happens, business is brought into the country from international sources, helping the economy.

Austria places a great influence on aiding the poor and less fortunate and helps them improve their lot in life. This is done through **income transfers**, such as welfare.

QUICK FACTS: THE ECONOMY OF AUSTRIA

Gross Domestic Product (GDP): $351.4 billion (2011 est.)

GDP per capita: $41,700 (2011 est.)

Industries: construction, machinery, vehicles and parts, food, metals, chemicals, lumber and wood processing, paper and paperboard, communications equipment, tourism

Agriculture: grains, potatoes, wine, fruit; dairy products, cattle, pigs, poultry; lumber

Export commodities: machinery and equipment, motor vehicles and parts, paper and paperboard, metal goods, chemicals, iron and steel, textiles, foodstuffs

Export partners: Germany 32.1%, Italy 7.9%, Switzerland 4.8%, France 4.2%, Czech Republic 4.1% (2010)

Import commodities: machinery and equipment, motor vehicles, chemicals, metal goods, oil and oil products; foodstuffs

Import partners: Germany 44%, Italy 6.8%, Switzerland 5.9%, Netherlands 4.1% (2010)

Currency: euro

Currency exchange rate: US $1= 0.7107 (2011 est.)

Note: All figures are from 2011 unless noted.
Source: www.cia.gov, 2012.

INDUSTRIES

Austria is highly industrialized and makes such goods as vehicle engines, as well as other electronic parts, like airbag chips and braking systems, for cars. However, the country is also known for the high percentage of its people who are employed by smaller companies. For example, many are involved in the craft-making industry. Austria is famous for handmade items like jewelry, ceramics, and blown glass. Tourism also contributes to the country's **gross domestic product (GDP)**, as people from all over the world visit this beautiful country.

While much of the economy consists of smaller businesses,

A busy city street

there are some large industries like iron and steel processing plants, as well as a large chemical manufacturing business. Other goods that are manufactured in Austria are lumber and processed wood, such as paper, computers and other communication equipment, and machinery.

Part of the reason that Austria is so prosperous is the abundance of raw materials from which the country can draw. The land is rich with deposits of iron and other important minerals buried deep below the earth's surface. Austria also has its own sources of oil and natural gas. As scientists work to end the world's dependence on oil, Austria is now generating **hydroelectric** power and is now the country that supplies the most to other members of the EU.

Austria's architecture draws tourists from around the world.

Imports and Exports

Altogether, Austria trades with over 150 countries; the member countries in the EU account for more than two-thirds of all exports. Most of these goods go to Germany, Italy, France, Switzerland, and Great Britain. The United States also trades with Austria. The country exports such things as machinery, motor vehicles, paper, chemicals, iron, fabrics, and food.

In return for these goods, Austria receives many others. These include chemicals, metal goods, oil, and mechanical equipment. Many of the goods are the same as those they import, and while this might seem **redundant**, there is a reason. When a country produces a good, they are also using up resources that might have been used in making different goods. Most of the time countries manufacture the goods with the least **opportunity costs**; this allows them to make as many things as possible. However, sometimes another country can make the same good cheaper; in other words, it has a **comparative advantage**. In that case, the two countries will trade.

Austrian Agriculture

About 18 percent of Austria is farmland. While this may not seem like a lot, about 5 percent of all people work in agriculture (compare this to the 1 percent of Americans who farm). The country also has about 20,000 **organic** farms, making it one of the most important countries in Europe for this type of agriculture.

Many foodstuffs are produced in Austria, including such things as grains, potatoes, and fruit. The country also has many dairy products as well as cattle, pigs, and poultry. Some of the fresh foods are made into other products such as wine.

Transportation

Austria has an efficient transportation system, with roads, waterways, airlines, and railroads all providing ways to get from one place to another. Vienna in particular has many ways to get around, including streetcars, subways, buses, and commuter trains. This transportation network not only serves to connect Austria's thriving economy; it also connects its people and culture.

Economic Challenge

Like the rest of the world, Austria has faced the economic recession that began in 2008 and continued on in the following years. However, because Austria's economy was so strong to start with, it did not experience as serious a problem as other countries in the EU. By 2010 and beyond, Austria appeared to be well on its way to economic recovery.

Visitors to one of Austria's museums

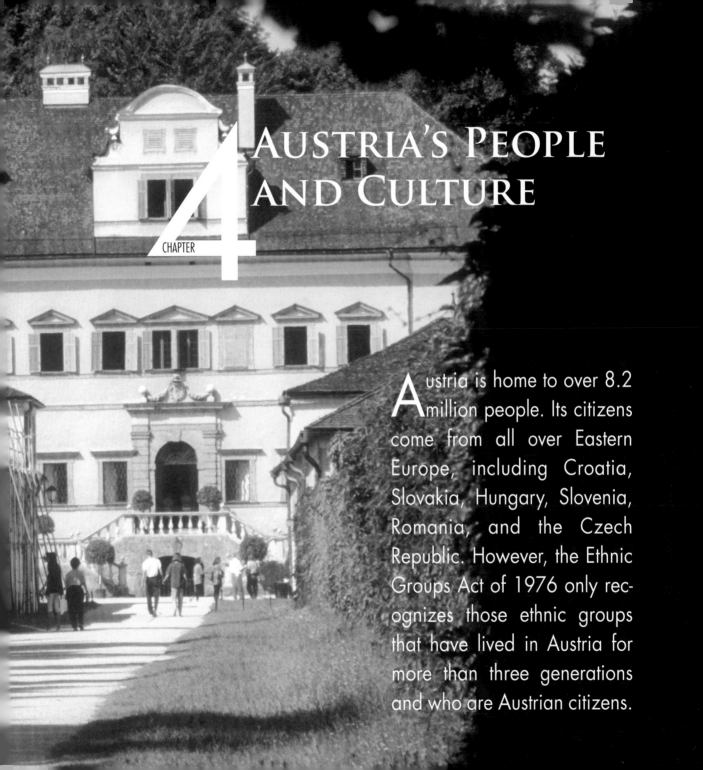

AUSTRIA'S PEOPLE AND CULTURE

CHAPTER 4

Austria is home to over 8.2 million people. Its citizens come from all over Eastern Europe, including Croatia, Slovakia, Hungary, Slovenia, Romania, and the Czech Republic. However, the Ethnic Groups Act of 1976 only recognizes those ethnic groups that have lived in Austria for more than three generations and who are Austrian citizens.

Salzburg's many churches reflect Austria's religious heritage.

These recognized ethic groups are scattered throughout Austria. In Burgenland are the Croatians and Hungarians. The Slovenians have made their home in the Gail, Rosen, and Jaun valleys in the south, while the Czechs and Slovaks live in Vienna and southern Austria.

No matter what the cultural background of Austrian citizens, they have one thing that ties most of them together: a common language. Ninety-eight percent of the population speaks German.

RELIGION

In Austria, there is a law that states everyone over fourteen is allowed to choose their own religion. However, the majority (about 78 percent) is Catholic. This stems from the old Hapsburg dynasty, which was a Catholic power. During the Hapsburg reign, the government persecuted all non-Catholics. It was not until 1867 that a policy of religious tolerance was put into place, and while everyone is now free to make their own decisions regarding religion, many cling to their old faith.

In 1908, the Austro-Hungarian Empire took control of Bosnia Herzegovina, with its large percentage of Muslims in the population. Because of this, Austria was the first in Europe to officially recognize the Muslim faith. Today, other religious minorities include Protestants, Buddhists, Mormons, Jews, and Greek-Orthodox.

Catholics are known for their religious education, but in Austria they are not the only providers of religious schools. Many smaller churches and other religious groups also offer education based on their faith. While in the United States these are private schools and paid for through tuition from the families who attend, in Austria all education—including religious education—is paid for by the state.

EDUCATION

The Austrian school system has been developing since Maria Theresa put forth the "General School Regulations," a set of guidelines for schools in 1774. Now all students must attend at least nine years of schooling, from the time they are six until age fourteen. If, after that, teens wish to drop out of school, they can attend a polytechnic course that will prepare them for a job.

School starts at the elementary level, which lasts for four years. After that, students attend secondary school. Once this level is completed, there are many choices teens and their families can make. One school is the *allgemein bildende höhere Sculen*, which is mostly general education, much like an American high school. Austrian students, however, can either focus on the arts or sciences. Vocational schools are another option, one that provides practical job training to students. After completing either of these types of course, students are issued a certificate much like a high school diploma, that allows the bearer to apply to a university.

Austrian education is nationally regulated, and all schools must hold to the same standards. However, some educators are working toward letting school districts have more freedom in creating their students' curriculum. All schools are free of charge, as are textbooks and transportation to and from school.

Quick Facts: The People of Austria

Population: 8,219,743 (July 2012 est.)

Ethnic groups: Austrians 91.1%, former Yugoslavs 4% (includes Croatians, Slovenes, Serbs, and Bosniaks), Turks 1.6%, German 0.9%, other or unspecified 2.4% (2001 census)

Age structure:
  0-14 years: 14%
  15-64 years: 67.7%
  65 years and above: 18.2%

Population growth rate: 0.14%

Birth rate: 8.69 births/1,000 population (2012 est.)

Death rate: 10.23 deaths/1,000 population (July 2012 est.)

Migration rate: 1.79 migrant(s)/1,000 population (2012 est.)

Infant mortality rate: 4.26 deaths/1,000 live births

Life expectancy at birth:
  Total population: 79.91 years
  Male: 77 years
  Female: 82.97 years (2012 est.)

Total fertility rate: 1.35 children born/woman

Religions: Roman Catholic 73.6%, Protestant 4.7%, Muslim 4.2%, other 0.1%, none 17.4%

Languages: Roman Catholic 73.6%, Protestant 4.7%, Muslim 4.2%, other 3.5%, unspecified 2%, none 12% (2001 census)

Literacy rate: 98%

Note: All figures are from 2011 unless otherwise noted.
Source: www.cia.gov, 2012.

Food

Reflecting the diverse population, Austrian food features a great variety of specialties, many of which are known throughout the world. Among these delicacies is *Weiner Schnitzel*, which is fried, breaded veal. Other popular Austrian dishes include *strudels* (or pies) and *Kaiserschmarrn*, a type of potato salad.

Music and Literature

Austria is very proud of the fact that it is the birthplace of Wolfgang Amadeus Mozart, the prolific composer who wrote hundreds of songs. Many other famous composers called Austria home as well, including Ludwig van Beethoven, Johannes Brahms, Joseph Haydn, Franz Schubert, Johann Strauss Sr. and Johann Strauss Jr. Not all of Austria's musicians lived hundreds of years ago; the country is also home to famous modern groups like Flaco and DJ Ötzi.

Austria has given birth to many famous literary figures as well. One such author, Joseph Roth, became well known for his portrayal of the downfall of the Hapsburg Empire. One of his novels, *Savoy Hotel*, tells of life in a hotel and shows it as a haven for people in trouble who are looking to escape.

Mozart's house

A Salzburg snack bar

Another Austrian author is Felix Salten. While the name may not sound familiar, he is the man behind the story *Bambi*, which was later turned into an animated movie by Walt Disney. Other literary figures include Ferdinand Raimond, Ingeborg Bachmann, and Peter Handke.

ARTS AND ARCHITECTURE

While many of the Austrian painters are less well known than some of the other artists of similar time periods, the country is still home to much artistic talent. One such artist is Gustav Klimt. Klimt's work dates from the late nineteenth century and is characterized by intensive colors and symbolism, as well as sometimes using a gold background. His work was very controversial at the time because of its **erotic** elements, but he has become very popular with Austrians today. Other Austrian painters include Egon Schiele (1890–1918), Oskar Kokoschka (1886–1980), and Friedensreich Hundertwasser (1928–2000).

Austrian architecture, especially in the city of Vienna, represents a diversity of time periods and styles. The country is a hodgepodge of different buildings, from the **baroque** to the **avant-garde** styles.

FESTIVALS AND EVENTS

Austria celebrates many festivals and events throughout the year, many of which are smaller, regional activities. Many of these center around music, with many festivals celebrating Austria's many composers. These provide a time to listen to and perform the music of such famous musicians as Mozart, Beethoven, and Strauss.

Austria also has many religious holidays, like Epiphany, Easter, St. Nicolas Day, and Christmas. Austrians celebrate All Souls Day on November 1 as a time to honor the dead. Children are given gifts and food while the souls are told that a tolling bell allows them to leave this earth.

These festivities are celebrated across Austria, but particularly in the cities, where most Austrians make their homes.

Three of the Most Famous Austrians

Sigmund Freud, *the father of psychoanalysis*
Wolfgang Puck, *celebrity chef*
Arnold Schwarzenegger, *actor and governor of California*

City of Vienna

5 CHAPTER LOOKING TO THE FUTURE

While there are many small villages and hamlets in Austria, most of the population lives in larger cities. Sixty-eight percent of people live in urban areas, while the others are spread out throughout the country. Family size in urban areas, as well as the rest of Austria, is relatively small, with most families only having one or two children.

Austria has come a long way. Less than sixty years ago, the country became independent after a nine-year occupation following World War II. Since then, Austria has certainly secured her place in the world. Austrians are enthusiastic about integrating EU policies, but the country has also led the way toward healthier trends for society, the environment, and the economy.

THE EUROPEAN UNION'S INFLUENCE

Austria has a long history, but it has only been part of the EU for a mere fraction of that time. The effects of joining the European Union, however, have been immense. Most of its recent economic success can be attributed to its membership in the EU. This is due to more than just increased trade.

The Common Agricultural Policy was originally created under the Treaties of Rome in 1957. It has changed drastically since that time, but over the years it has helped regulate the agricultural industry across all nations involved. Austria's agricultural products include grains, potatoes, dairy, meat, vegetables, fruit, and wine. Although agriculture is not even close to being the greatest source of Austria's income, this particular policy has helped protect the jobs of many farmers in the nation.

Despite the benefits, some Austrians are finding it difficult to accept the changes caused as a result of joining the EU. As is the case with other issues as well, being a member of the EU requires that Austria's government give up some of its power in order to follow the policies set forth by the union. Some people, used to being completely independent, dislike handing over their power to an international organization. This tension has become particularly noticeable in the past few years during large shifts in political power.

SOCIAL AND CULTURAL IMPLICATIONS

Austria's economic success has also caused an increased interest in the importance of art and culture. Starting in 2009, the budget for art and culture was increased by 50 million euros.

The budget increase will be used to support a new generation of contemporary art, improve working conditions in cultural fields, and teach the arts in schools. Also, general funding has been increased to aid theaters, museums, libraries, and the film industry. New policies have been put into place to protect historical buildings, monuments, and other forms of cultural heritage, as well.

If Austria's current trend of economic recovery continues, funding for these cultural programs will likely continue to increase as well. This will not only preserve Austria's cultural heritage, but will

The natural history museum in Vienna, Austria.

also encourage the creation of new works of art and culture.

Austria also supports legislation that protects the rights of all human beings. Discrimination and prejudice against Roma, Turks, and other groups continue to be a reality, but the government is working hard to promote tolerance and equal rights for all human beings within Austria's borders.

Education is one way to do this. College education is now given to all Austrian citizens free of charge. Between 2001 and 2008, students were charged 363.36 euros per semester (about $490, a tiny fraction of the cost of college in the United

Austria gets almost 60 percent of their energy from renewable energy sources, such as these wind turbines.

States) to attend an Austrian university. This fee was dropped in 2009, allowing anyone from a EU member country to attend a university in Austria free of charge. The only exception is if a student spends more time than expected at the university. A student may attend university for two semesters after the recommended graduation time, but if the student attends for longer than this, she is required to pay the fee. This encourages students to graduate on time, and helps ensure that the money used to fund this privilege is not wasted.

A free education means a brighter future and further advances for the country. Austria's policies allow a person from any background the chance to be just as successful as anyone else. And unlike countries such as the United States, attending university in Austria will not put you in debt for years to come!

ENERGY CONSERVATION

Austria is one of only a few countries that get more than 50 percent of their energy from renewable energy sources. Over half the electricity in Austria is generated through the use of hydroelectric power. Together with wind, biomass, geothermal and solar power, renewable energy sources make up almost 60 percent of all electrical energy consumed in Austria. Due to a law passed several decades ago, the use of nuclear power is forbidden in Austria.

The policies of the European Union require member countries to work toward certain standards. Austria is leading the way in development for cleaner energy.

FUTURE HIGHLIGHTS

In 2012, Austria hosts the first Youth Winter Olympics, for athletes between the ages of fourteen and eighteen. The games will be held in Innsbruck, a city in the western part of Austria. In the past, Innsbruck has hosted Olympic Games in 1964 and in 1976. The city has also hosted the 1984 and 1988 Paralympics. Austria was chosen to host the Youth Winter Olympics partly because the organizers know the country had the expertise to host an Olympic event. In addition, Austria's financial stability means they will make a successful Olympic host.

As a member of the European Union, Austria is thriving and stable. The people of Austria face many challenges—but they look toward a bright tomorrow, ready to face whatever lies ahead.

Time Line

80,000–10,000 BCE	Austria is settled.
0	The Romans control the land that is now Austria.
700 CE	Charlemagne takes over the territory.
900s	Magyars from Hungary attack and conquer Austria.
955	Otto the Great vanquishes the Magyars.
1500s	The Ottoman Empire invades.
1600s	The Ottomans are defeated.
1618	The Protestants rebel against the Catholic Hapsburg emperor, leading to the Thirty Years' War.
1648	The Peace of Westphalia ends the war, making Austria a Roman Catholic nation.
1701–1714	Austria and France fight the War of Spanish Succession (Austria wins Belgium and Spain's Italian lands).
Late 1700s–1815	The Napoleonic Wars.
1815	Napoleon is defeated.
1859	Austria declares war on Sardinia and is defeated by Italy and France.
1867	The Austro-Hungarian Empire comes into being.
1914	Archduke Franz Ferdinand is assassinated and World War I starts.
November 3, 1918	World War I ends.
November 12, 1918	The last Hapsburg emperor is overthrown and the Austrian republic is formed.
1938	Hitler seizes control of Austria.
October 1939	World War II starts.
1945	The Allies defeat Germany.
1945	Austrian territory is divided between the United States, Britain, France, and the Soviet Union.
1954	The occupation of Austria ends.
January 1, 1995	Austria joins the EU.
2008	Recession hits the global economy.
2012	Austria hosts the first Youth Winter Olympics.

Further Reading/Internet Resources

In Books

Allport, Alan. *Austria*. New York: Chelsea House, 2002.

Merino, Noel. *The European Union*. Farmington Hills, Mich.: Greenhaven Press, 2008.

Roman, Eric. *Austria-Hungary and the Successor States: A Reference Guide from the Renaissance to the Present*. New York: Facts On File, 2003.

Staab, Andreas. *The European Union Explained: Institutions, Actors, Global Impact*. Bloomington: University of Indiana Press, 2008.

Stein, R. Conrad. *Austria*. New York: Scholastic Library Publishing, 2000.

On the Internet

Austria: CIA World Factbook
www.cia.gov/library/publications/the-world-factbook/geos/au.html

Austria: Country Studies
lcweb2.loc.gov/frd/cs/attoc.html

Austria Travel Information and Travel Guide
www.lonelyplanet.com/austria

Austrian National Tourism Office
www.austriatourism.com

Information and Services of the City of Vienna
www.wien.gv.at/english/

The Official Website of the European Union
europa.eu/index_en.htm

Glossary

anarchy: Absence of any formal system of government.

anti-Semitism: Policies, views, or actions that harm or discriminate against Jewish people.

atrocities: Shockingly cruel acts of violence, especially during war.

avant-garde: Artistically new, experimental, or unconventional.

baroque: A highly ornamental style of European art and architecture.

capitalist: Follower of an economic system based on private ownership of the means of production and distribution of goods, characterized by a free competitive market and the profit motive.

Celtic: Relating to someone who belonged to an ancient Indo-European people of pre-Roman time, who lived in central and western Europe.

coalition: The temporary union between two or more groups.

comparative advantage: When one country can produce something cheaper than another country.

constitution: The written document setting out the fundamental laws of a country.

currency: The bills and coins used as money in a particular country.

discrimination: Unfair treatment of a minority group.

economies: Communities' production and consumption of goods and services.

erotic: Arousing, or designed to arouse, feelings of sexual desire.

fascism: A system of government characterized by dictatorship, centralized control of private enterprise, elimination of opposition, and extreme nationalism.

freedom of the press: The right of the press to report on matters without fear of reprisals.

gross domestic product (GDP): The total value of all goods and services produced within a country in a year.

hydroelectric: Relating to the generation of electricity by means of water pressure.

income transfers: Government payments to individuals meeting certain criteria, such as low income.

militias: Armies composed of civilian soldiers.

nationalism: A strong sense of patriotism and loyalty for one's country.

opportunity costs: The added costs of using resources that is the difference between the actual value that results from those costs and that of an alternative use of those resources.

organic: Grown without artificial supplements or pesticides.

parliament: A house of government.

permeated: Entered something and spread throughout it completely.

police system: The use of the police, especially secret police, by a government to exercise strict control over a population.

precursor: Somebody or something that comes before, and is considered to lead to the development, of another person or thing.

privatize: To transfer state ownership of an economic enterprise or public utility into private ownership.

Protestant Revolution: A reaction to Catholicism characterized by the expansion of Protestantism.

provisional government: A government that is temporary or conditional, pending confirmation or validation.

radical: Favoring sweeping or extreme economic, political, or social changes.

recession: A period of economic slowdown.

redundant: Repetitive, unnecessary.

reparations: Compensations for wrongs.

repression: The condition of having political, social, or cultural freedom controlled by force.

right: Political conservatism.

secularization: The act of transferring something from a religious to a nonreligious use.

serfdom: The feudal European practice of having an agricultural worker cultivate land belonging to a landowner and who was bought and sold with the land.

socialist: A follower of the political theory or system in which the means of production and distribution are controlled by the people and operated according to fairness rather than market principles.

succession: The assumption of a position or title, the right to take it up, or the order in which it is taken up.

tariff: A tax levied by a government on goods, usually imports.

toleration: Official acceptance by a government of religious beliefs and practices that are different from the ones it holds.

totalitarian: Relating to a centralized government system in which a single party without opposition rules over political, economic, social, and cultural life.

trafficking: Dealing or traiding something illegal.

vanquished: Defeated convincingly.

xenophobic: Having an intense fear or dislike of foreign people, their customs and culture.

INDEX

Picture Credits

About the Authors and the Consultant

Authors

Jeanine Sanna lives in upstate New York with a variety of animals. In addition to being an author and journalist, she is interested in the field of forensic chemistry. Jeanine also enjoys traveling, music, and theater.

Shaina Carmel Indovino is a writer and illustrator living in Nesconset, New York. She graduated from Binghamton University, where she received degrees in sociology and English. Shaina has enjoyed the opportunity to apply both of her fields of study to her writing and she hopes readers will benefit from taking a look at the countries of the world through more than one perspective.

Series Consultant

Ambassador John Bruton served as Irish Prime Minister from 1994 until 1997. As prime minister, he helped turn Ireland's economy into one of the fastest-growing in the world. He was also involved in the Northern Ireland Peace Process, which led to the 1998 Good Friday Agreement. During his tenure as Ireland's prime minister, he also presided over the European Union presidency in 1996 and helped finalize the Stability and Growth Pact, which governs management of the euro. Before being named the European Commission Head of Delegation in the United States, he was a member of the convention that drafted the European Constitution, signed October 29, 2004.

The European Commission Delegation to the United States represents the interests of the European Union as a whole, much as ambassadors represent their countries' interests to the U.S. government. Matters coming under European Commission authority are negotiated between the commission and the U.S. administration.